The
Good
Seed
Guide

**All you need to know
about growing trees from seed**

THE TREE COUNCIL

THE ALLIANCE FOR
BEVERAGE CARTONS
AND THE ENVIRONMENT

The Tree Council is a national registered charity, founded in 1974, which promotes the planting and conservation of trees and woods in town and country throughout the United Kingdom. Its members include over 150 organisations concerned with trees.

Each year the Tree Council organises a series of campaigns designed to help people enjoy trees. These include:

Seed Gathering Sunday - a time to collect tree seeds for future planting, on the second Sunday in October each year. Made possible by the Alliance for Beverage Cartons and the Environment.

National Tree Week- the annual launch of the tree planting season, from late November until the first weekend of December. Supported by Esso, a subsidiary of ExxonMobil.

Trees Love Care (TLC) - a campaign focusing on the essential aftercare of newly-planted trees. March to September.

Center Parcs Walk in the Woods - walks and events in woods throughout May each year, when they are at their best.

The Tree Council also organises the **National Grid Tree Warden Scheme**, which co-ordinates trained volunteers who play an active role in conserving their local trees and woods. To find out if there is a Tree Warden Scheme in your area, contact The Tree Council.

The Tree Council
71 Newcomen Street
London SE1 1YT
☎ 020 7407 9992 Fax: 020 7407 9908
info@treecouncil.org.uk
www.treecouncil.org.uk

The Tree Council

THE TREE COUNCIL

Planting a tree is something simple that everybody can do to benefit the environment.

Trees are an essential part of the world ecosystem: producing oxygen and storing carbon dioxide, making and conserving soil, affecting climate and weather, and supporting myriad forms of wildlife.

In our towns and cities they are beneficial to health, as they filter dust and pollutants from the air and reduce stress levels, increasing feelings of calm and well-being. They are also beautiful and provide a link with nature and the seasons.

Young trees can be bought from a garden centre or nursery. However, a more interesting and rewarding way is to collect tree seed and grow your own. You are also helping to perpetuate your local tree species.

This book is designed to give you the information you need to identify, collect, grow and plant your own trees, in an easy-to-follow format that should guarantee success.

The Tree Council has designated the second Sunday in October as Seed Gathering Sunday. We hope you will join in with this nationwide day of action to find your own tree seeds. But if you can't join us on that day, please use this guide to do your own thing, in your own time, and plant trees for the planet and its people.

Caroline Davis
Chairman/Tree Council

ACE

**THE ALLIANCE FOR
BEVERAGE CARTONS
AND THE ENVIRONMENT**

The Alliance for Beverage Cartons and the Environment is an international group of companies that make paperboard and cartons and strive to protect the environment.

The Alliance for Beverage Cartons and the Environment is an international group of companies that make paperboard and cartons and strive to protect the environment.

One of the aims of the Alliance is to help people make the connection between cartons and trees and to understand the environmental benefits of choosing a renewable, rather than a finite, resource.

The beverage carton is the only drinks package made with an infinitely renewable raw material trees. Between 75-90% of the carton is paperboard, predominantly twigs and offcuts from pine and spruce trees planted for timber. This is coated with a fine layer of polyethylene to make it watertight and, for long-life drinks, an additional very thin layer of aluminium, less than the width of a human hair, which protects the contents without the need for refrigeration or preservatives.

Concern for the preservation of ancient British oaks and the well-being of Nordic spruce and pine forests are not incompatible. Alliance members take seriously the responsibility for sustainable management of their forests in Northern Europe, growing trees with respect for biodiversity and the natural cycle. At every harvest, care is taken to plant more trees than are felled.

The Alliance for Beverage Cartons and the Environment,
3 - 5 Latimer Road, Teddington, Middlesex TW11 8QA
Tel 0208 977 6116
Fax 0208 977 6909
Press Office 01434 602899
www.drinkscartons.com

The Carbon Cycle

Through photosynthesis, trees take carbon dioxide from the air, nutrients and water from the ground and, using energy from the sun, produce wood. When wood and forest products are burned or decay, the carbon dioxide is once again released as part of the natural carbon cycle. The ability of growing forests to capture carbon dioxide helps, in some measure, to offset the greenhouse effect.

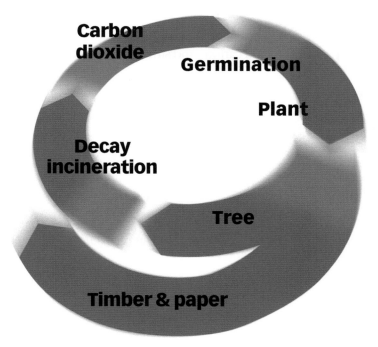

Carbon dioxide

Germination

Plant

Decay incineration

Tree

Timber & paper

In Northern Europe the standing forest which supplies trees for liquid packaging board, is actually increasing year after year as more trees are planted than felled. In the UK, The Alliance for Beverage Cartons & the Environment supports tree-planting initiatives, particularly those that help people make the connection between paper cartons and trees.

Identifying Trees and Collecting Their Seeds

The first section of this book is designed to help you to identify trees and their seeds in your garden, or out in the woods and fields.

The species included in this book are either native to, or commonly found in, the British Isles. We have divided their fruits and seeds into four main groups: Nuts, Fleshy Fruits, Winged Seeds and Cones. The exception to this arrangement are the willows and poplars, which do produce seeds but are most conveniently propagated by taking cuttings from the parent tree. (See p.44-47)

For each species of tree, this book gives you:

- Basic facts about the tree, such as where it is commonly found, what its wood is used for, and the wildlife that the tree supports.

- Instructions about how to collect the seeds and how to grow them.

- Specific identification features for the seeds and leaves.

- An outline silhouette for each tree, with figures showing the average height of the tree at 5 years, 10 years and maturity.

- Where trees have similar leaf shapes, we have suggested other species you should check in order to avoid misidentification.

- A time-bar that shows you when to collect, stratify, sow, grow and plant out each tree species. Stratification, which is mentioned in the text, is explained in detail on p.

Look at the second section of the book for further, more detailed instructions about how to prepare, germinate, grow and plant each species.

Cones

This group of trees have seeds contained in a cone (eg. pines) or conelike structures (eg. alders and birches).

Winged seeds

This group, as the name suggests, produces seeds that have 'wings' attached to them.

Nuts

This group includes trees and shrubs which produce genuine nuts, as well as those that produce nut-like seeds.

Fleshy Fruits

This group is arranged in the following order: trees that produce red berries and fruits first, followed by black berries, and finally apples and pears.

English Oak - *Quercus robur*

Large tree (5:10:35)

The English oak is a native tree of woodlands, hedgerows and parkland in many parts of Britain. It grows best on deep fertile clays and loams but will tolerate a wide range of soils. Some of the largest oaks in Britain are thought to be over 1,000 years old.

The oak has always been the most widely used hardwood in Britain and its hard, durable timber has traditionally been used for buildings, ships, furniture, panelling and coffins.

The English oak supports some 500 species of invertebrates, more than any other species of British tree. The purple hairstreak butterfly breeds solely on this and other species of oak, and small groups of them can often be seen fluttering over the treetops in mid-July to late August. The oak is also used by birds and bats as roosting and nesting sites.

Seed Guide: Collect the acorns from the tree or as soon as possible after they drop - usually from late September onwards. Separate acorns from their cups and float them in a bucket of water; plant the ones that sink. To avoid your acorns drying out - which will kill them - sow straightaway in a seedbed to a depth of 10cms, or singly, in pots, covered by a thin layer of compost. Protect from predators throughout the winter. Roots will grow during the winter and the shoots will emerge in late April.

The leaves are almost stalkless. The acorns have long stalks.

Easily confused with: Sessile Oak, Turkey Oak and other oak species.

	JAN	FEB	MAR	APR	MAY	JUN	JUL	AUG	SEP	OCT	NOV	DEC
Year 1									Collect			
									Sow			
Year 2				Grow						Plant		
Year 3												

Sessile Oak - *Quercus petraea*

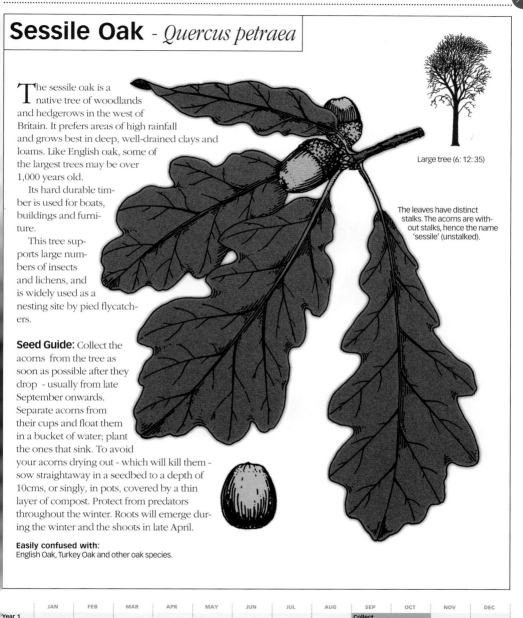

The sessile oak is a native tree of woodlands and hedgerows in the west of Britain. It prefers areas of high rainfall and grows best in deep, well-drained clays and loams. Like English oak, some of the largest trees may be over 1,000 years old.

Its hard durable timber is used for boats, buildings and furniture.

This tree supports large numbers of insects and lichens, and is widely used as a nesting site by pied flycatchers.

Large tree (6: 12: 35)

The leaves have distinct stalks. The acorns are without stalks, hence the name 'sessile' (unstalked).

Seed Guide: Collect the acorns from the tree as soon as possible after they drop - usually from late September onwards. Separate acorns from their cups and float them in a bucket of water; plant the ones that sink. To avoid your acorns drying out - which will kill them - sow straightaway in a seedbed to a depth of 10cms, or singly, in pots, covered by a thin layer of compost. Protect from predators throughout the winter. Roots will emerge during the winter and the shoots in late April.

Easily confused with:
English Oak, Turkey Oak and other oak species.

	JAN	FEB	MAR	APR	MAY	JUN	JUL	AUG	SEP	OCT	NOV	DEC
Year 1									Collect			
									Sow			
Year 2			Grow							Plant		
Year 3												

Turkey Oak - *Quercus cerris*

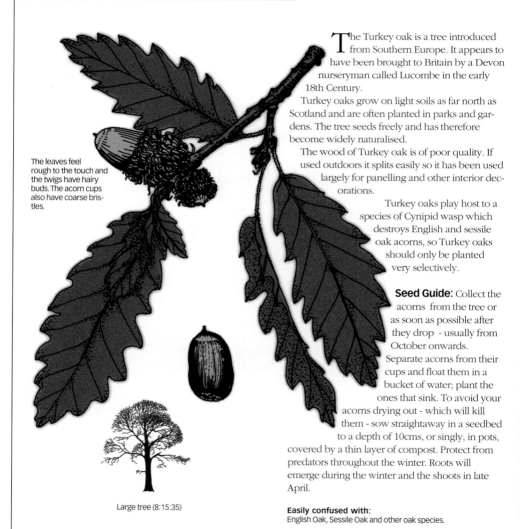

The leaves feel rough to the touch and the twigs have hairy buds. The acorn cups also have coarse bristles.

Large tree (8:15:35)

The Turkey oak is a tree introduced from Southern Europe. It appears to have been brought to Britain by a Devon nurseryman called Lucombe in the early 18th Century.

Turkey oaks grow on light soils as far north as Scotland and are often planted in parks and gardens. The tree seeds freely and has therefore become widely naturalised.

The wood of Turkey oak is of poor quality. If used outdoors it splits easily so it has been used largely for panelling and other interior decorations.

Turkey oaks play host to a species of Cynipid wasp which destroys English and sessile oak acorns, so Turkey oaks should only be planted very selectively.

Seed Guide: Collect the acorns from the tree or as soon as possible after they drop - usually from October onwards.

Separate acorns from their cups and float them in a bucket of water; plant the ones that sink. To avoid your acorns drying out - which will kill them - sow straightaway in a seedbed to a depth of 10cms, or singly, in pots, covered by a thin layer of compost. Protect from predators throughout the winter. Roots will emerge during the winter and the shoots in late April.

Easily confused with:
English Oak, Sessile Oak and other oak species.

	JAN	FEB	MAR	APR	MAY	JUN	JUL	AUG	SEP	OCT	NOV	DEC
Year 1										Collect		
										Sow		
Year 2				Grow						Plant		
Year 3												

Beech - *Fagus sylvatica*

Large tree (6:10:35)

The beech is the dominant native species on chalk and limestone. It prefers well-drained soils but can be found in heavy clays. It has been widely planted in parks and gardens as well as extensively used for hedging.

The wood is strong and tough and was used for tool handles and flooring and is still widely used for kitchen utensils and children's toys. The beech mast (nuts) was also used as pig feed.

The dense shade cast by beechwoods means that they have a restricted but specialised flora, including bird's-nest orchid, the rare ghost orchid and various helleborines. Some 94 species of invertebrates have been found in beech trees, including the lobster and barred hooked-tip moths.

Oval leaves with a wavy margin. The seeds are contained in a brown husk.

Seed Guide: Check the first fall of beech-nuts in autumn – they may be empty. Collect only plump, ripe nuts from the ground. Sow immediately in a pot or seedbed; protect from predators and severe frost.

Easily confused with: Hornbeam.

	JAN	FEB	MAR	APR	MAY	JUN	JUL	AUG	SEP	OCT	NOV	DEC
Year 1									Collect			Stratify
									Sow			Stratify
Year 2				Grow						Plant		
Year 3												

Horse Chestnut - *Aesculus hippocastanum*

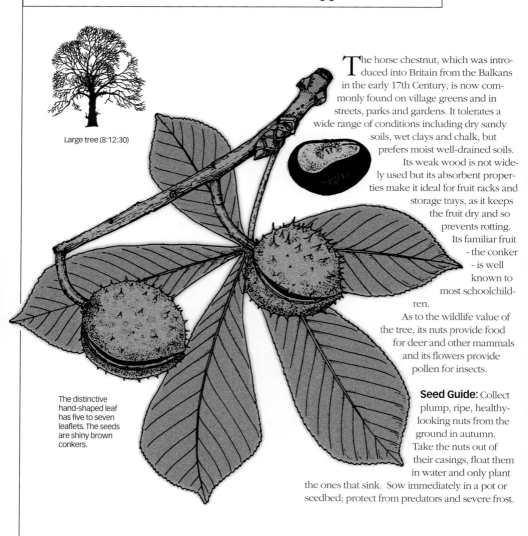

Large tree (8:12:30)

The distinctive hand-shaped leaf has five to seven leaflets. The seeds are shiny brown conkers.

The horse chestnut, which was introduced into Britain from the Balkans in the early 17th Century, is now commonly found on village greens and in streets, parks and gardens. It tolerates a wide range of conditions including dry sandy soils, wet clays and chalk, but prefers moist well-drained soils. Its weak wood is not widely used but its absorbent properties make it ideal for fruit racks and storage trays, as it keeps the fruit dry and so prevents rotting. Its familiar fruit - the conker - is well known to most schoolchildren.

As to the wildlife value of the tree, its nuts provide food for deer and other mammals and its flowers provide pollen for insects.

Seed Guide: Collect plump, ripe, healthy-looking nuts from the ground in autumn. Take the nuts out of their casings, float them in water and only plant the ones that sink. Sow immediately in a pot or seedbed; protect from predators and severe frost.

	JAN	FEB	MAR	APR	MAY	JUN	JUL	AUG	SEP	OCT	NOV	DEC
Year 1									Collect			Stratify
									Sow			Stratify
Year 2				Grow						Plant		
Year 3												

Sweet Chestnut - *Castanea sativa*

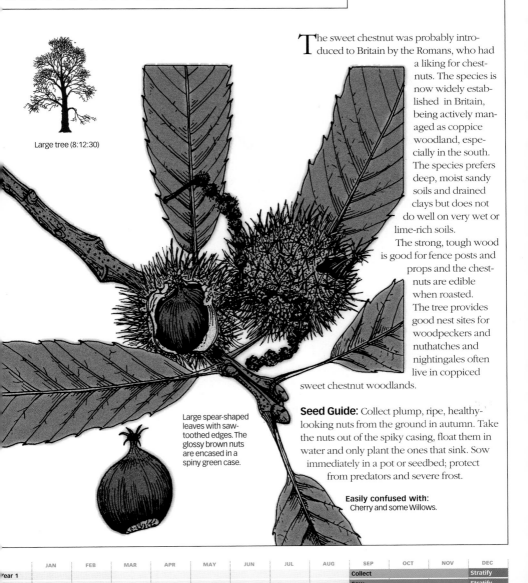

Large tree (8:12:30)

The sweet chestnut was probably introduced to Britain by the Romans, who had a liking for chestnuts. The species is now widely established in Britain, being actively managed as coppice woodland, especially in the south. The species prefers deep, moist sandy soils and drained clays but does not do well on very wet or lime-rich soils.

The strong, tough wood is good for fence posts and props and the chestnuts are edible when roasted. The tree provides good nest sites for woodpeckers and nuthatches and nightingales often live in coppiced sweet chestnut woodlands.

Large spear-shaped leaves with saw-toothed edges. The glossy brown nuts are encased in a spiny green case.

Seed Guide: Collect plump, ripe, healthy-looking nuts from the ground in autumn. Take the nuts out of the spiky casing, float them in water and only plant the ones that sink. Sow immediately in a pot or seedbed; protect from predators and severe frost.

Easily confused with:
Cherry and some Willows.

	JAN	FEB	MAR	APR	MAY	JUN	JUL	AUG	SEP	OCT	NOV	DEC
Year 1									Collect			Stratify
									Sow			Stratify
Year 2				Grow					Plant			
Year 3												

Walnut - *Juglans regia*

The walnut was probably introduced into Britain by the Romans and has subsequently become widespread in southern and central England. Further north it is found largely in parks and gardens. The tree grows best on well-drained soils, especially clays.

Often called the 'king of timbers', this hardwood was used to make aeroplane propellers and is still used for cabinet making, decorative veneers and rifle butts.

The foliage of walnut gives off a scent similar to shoe polish and a sprig kept in a jar is said to deter flies. The walnut itself is widely eaten by humans, either pickled or raw. Rooks also like them and many trees grow from walnuts buried and forgotten by these birds.

Seed Guide: Collect the fruits, from the tree or ground, as soon as the husks darken or turn black. Remove husks and sow immediately in a pot or seedbed; protect from predators and severe frost.

Easily confused with:
Ash, Elder, Rowan.

Each large leaf has seven leaflets which get larger towards the tip. The round green fruit contains the familiar wrinkled brown nut.

Large tree (8:15:30)

	JAN	FEB	MAR	APR	MAY	JUN	JUL	AUG	SEP	OCT	NOV	DEC
Year 1										Collect		Stratify
										Sow		Stratify
Year 2				Grow						Plant		
Year 3												

Hazel - *Corylus avellana*

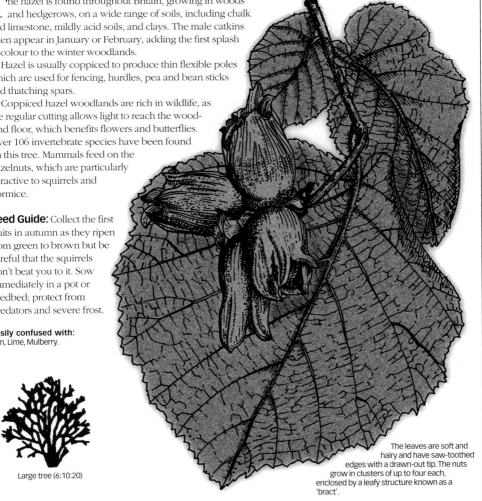

The hazel is found throughout Britain, growing in woods and hedgerows, on a wide range of soils, including chalk and limestone, mildly acid soils, and clays. The male catkins often appear in January or February, adding the first splash of colour to the winter woodlands.

Hazel is usually coppiced to produce thin flexible poles which are used for fencing, hurdles, pea and bean sticks and thatching spars.

Coppiced hazel woodlands are rich in wildlife, as the regular cutting allows light to reach the woodland floor, which benefits flowers and butterflies. Over 106 invertebrate species have been found on this tree. Mammals feed on the hazelnuts, which are particularly attractive to squirrels and dormice.

Seed Guide: Collect the first fruits in autumn as they ripen from green to brown but be careful that the squirrels don't beat you to it. Sow immediately in a pot or seedbed; protect from predators and severe frost.

Easily confused with:
Elm, Lime, Mulberry.

Large tree (6:10:20)

The leaves are soft and hairy and have saw-toothed edges with a drawn-out tip. The nuts grow in clusters of up to four each, enclosed by a leafy structure known as a 'bract'.

	JAN	FEB	MAR	APR	MAY	JUN	JUL	AUG	SEP	OCT	NOV	DEC
Year 1									Collect		Stratify	
									Sow		Stratify	
Year 2			Grow							Plant		
Year 3												

Holly - *Ilex aquifolium*

Medium tree: (4:6:20)

Shiny evergreen leaves have a waxy upperside and spiny edges. Only the female trees have the bright red berries.

The holly is a very widespread native tree which grows on almost any soil. It tolerates shade well, often grows as the understorey in woodlands but also like open situations and occurs widely in hedgerows.

Its hard, white wood takes stain well and was traditionally known as 'English ebony'. It was particularly used for carving and inlay, whilst the shoots with berries are used for Christmas decorations.

The berries are eaten by birds, the foliage by deer and rabbits. Holly is also the foodplant of the holly blue butterfly, but only nine other invertebrate species have been found feeding on this tree.

Seed Guide: Collect the ripe, red berries from the tree in winter. Remove the seeds from the flesh and wash them thoroughly. Soak the berries for a day or two if the flesh is hard to remove. Stratify the seed for one or more winters. Select and sow germinating seeds each spring.

	JAN	FEB	MAR	APR	MAY	JUN	JUL	AUG	SEP	OCT	NOV	DEC
Year 1										Collect		Stratify
Year 2			CHECK	CHECK								
Year 3			Sow		Grow							
Year 4										Plant		

Yew - *Taxus baccata*

The needles of the tree are dark green on their upperside and a lighter green underneath. The red fleshy fruit contains a dark single seed.

Medium tree (2:4:20)

The oldest tree in Britain is probably a yew growing in the churchyard of Fortingall, Perthshire, thought to be 5,000 years old. Many other ancient yews can be found in churchyards throughout Britain.

In the wild, yew prefer lime-rich soils and can, along with beech, become the dominant woodland type.

Its hard, colourful wood has an excellent finish and is used for a wide range of ornamental furniture, cabinets and bowls. Historically, yew produced the finest longbows, enabling archers to fire arrows over considerable distances.

The wildlife value of this species is limited, as the tree casts deep shade and few plants grow underneath it. The tree itself only supports a limited number of insects and is eaten by wild mammals. Birds also eat the red berries through the winter.

Seed Guide: Collect fruit from the tree when the outer berry is a bright red colour. Remember the seed contained within the red flesh is poisonous. Remove flesh and stratify the seed for at least two winters. Select and sow germinating seeds in early spring of the second and successive years. Yew seeds take a long time to stratify, and the seedlings are also very slow growing.

	JAN	FEB	MAR	APR	MAY	JUN	JUL	AUG	SEP	OCT	NOV	DEC
Year 1									Collect		Stratify	
Year 2			CHECK	CHECK								
Year 3			Sow		Grow							
Year 4											Plant	

Hawthorn - *Crataegus monogyna*

The native hawthorn grows throughout Britain, except in the extreme north-west of Scotland. It tolerates most soils except peat and is probably best known as a plant of hedgerows.

The wood has been used for tool handles and walking sticks and also produces excellent firewood and charcoal. The berries can be made into jellies, chutneys and wine.

The species has a high wildlife value, as its flowers provide nectar for spring insects and its berries provide excellent food for small mammals and birds, especially thrushes. Over 209 invertebrate species have been recorded living on this tree.

Seed Guide: Collect the red berries, once they are ripe, from autumn onwards. Remove the seeds from the flesh and wash them thoroughly. Soak the berries for a day or two, if the flesh is hard to remove. Stratify the seed, occasionally for one but usually two winters. Select and sow germinating seeds each spring.

Easily confused with:
Field Maple, Midland Hawthorn.

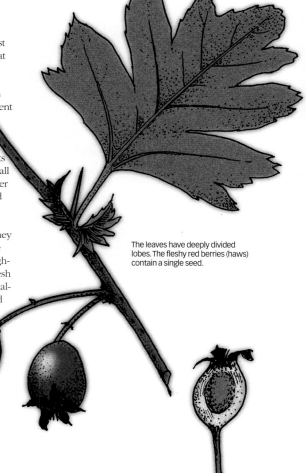

The leaves have deeply divided lobes. The fleshy red berries (haws) contain a single seed.

Usually seen as a shrub, but can be a medium tree (5:8:10)

	JAN	FEB	MAR	APR	MAY	JUN	JUL	AUG	SEP	OCT	NOV	DEC
Year 1									Collect		Stratify	
Year 2			CHECK	CHECK								
Year 3			Sow		Grow						Plant	
Year 4												

Midland Hawthorn - *Crataegus laevigata*

Medium tree (6:8:10)

Midland hawthorn is the rarer of the two native hawthorn species and the one that is more likely to grow into a small tree. It is found on heavy soils in shady woodlands, or growing along road-sides and in gardens, usually in the south east of Britain. Many ornamental forms have been created, including 'Paul's Scarlet', which is frequently seen in towns and cities.

As with hawthorn, the wood has been used for tool handles and walking sticks, its fluted stems making it particularly useful for the latter. The berries can be made into jellies, chutneys and wine.

The flowers provide nectar for spring insects, the berries excellent food for small mammals and birds, especially thrushes.

Seed Guide: Collect the red berries, once they are ripe, from autumn onwards. Remove the seeds from the flesh and wash them thoroughly. Soak the berries for a day or two, if the flesh is hard to remove. Stratify the seed, occasionally for one, but usually two, winters. Select and sow germinating seeds each spring.

Easily confused with: Hawthorn, Field Maple.

Leaves have shallower lobes than hawthorn and the red haws contain two seeds.

	JAN	FEB	MAR	APR	MAY	JUN	JUL	AUG	SEP	OCT	NOV	DEC
Year 1									Collect		Stratify	
Year 2			CHECK	CHECK								
Year 3			Sow		Grow					Plant		
Year 4												

Whitebeam - *Sorbus aria*

The whitebeam is a native tree which prefers chalk and lime-rich soils but it also tolerates other soil types. Its ability to withstand pollution means it has become a widely-planted urban tree, but such trees are often ornamental forms of the wild species and are unlikely to produce reasonable seed.

Its hard, tough wood was used to make machinery cogs. Its overripe berries can be turned into jelly to accompany venison. Whitebeam was also planted as a boundary marker; the white underside of its leaves, flashing in the wind, drew attention to the tree.

The leaves have a covering of thick white hairs underneath. The berries, which are at first green, ripen to bright red.

As with all Sorbus trees, the berries are eaten by birds, while the flowers attract insects and white caterpillars of the tiny moth Argynesthia sorbiella which feeds on the shoots and flower buds.

Seed Guide: Collect bunches of fruits when they turn crimson. Remove the seeds from the flesh and wash thoroughly. Stratify the seed, usually for one winter. In cool autumns, germination can be improved by keeping stratifying seeds at room temperature for two weeks, before putting them outside for the winter. Select and sow germinating seeds in spring.

Easily confused with:
Some Sorbus species, particularly Swedish Whitebeam.

Medium tree (5:8:15)

	JAN	FEB	MAR	APR	MAY	JUN	JUL	AUG	SEP	OCT	NOV	DEC
Year 1									Collect	Stratify		
Year 2			Sow	Grow						Plant		
Year 3												

Rowan - *Sorbus aucuparia*

Rowan is found throughout Britain, growing naturally at altitudes of up to 1,000m in Scotland. It is a tree of mountains, woodlands and valleys, growing on a wide range of soils including chalks, acid soils and even peat. It has been widely planted in parks, gardens and streets due to its striking red berries (which occur as early as July) and its autumn foliage.

Its timber is strong, hard and flexible, leading to its use in tools, carving and for shortbows, which were favoured mainly by the Welsh. The berries can be made into a jelly, which is excellent with cold game or wildfowl, and into a wholesome 'perry' or cider.

The tree has excellent wildlife value, providing fruit for thrushes and blackbirds, which in turn help the tree to colonise new areas by eating the seeds and dispersing them around the countryside.

Seed Guide: To beat the birds, collect the ripening clusters of berries from late August. Carefully remove the seeds from the flesh and wash thoroughly. Stratify the seed, usually for one winter. In cool autumns, germination can be improved by keeping stratifying seeds at room temperature for two weeks, before putting them outside for the winter. Select and sow germinating seeds in spring.

Each leaf consists of numerous pairs of stalkless leaflets. It has distinctive red berries.

Easily confused with:
Ash, Elder, Walnut.

Medium tree (8:12:15)

	JAN	FEB	MAR	APR	MAY	JUN	JUL	AUG	SEP	OCT	NOV	DEC
Year 1								Collect		Stratify		
Year 2			Sow	Grow						Plant		
Year 3												

Wild Service Tree - *Sorbus torminalis*

The wild service tree is the rarer woodland relative of rowan and whitebeam, appearing to germinate only in areas of ancient woodland, for which it is an indicator. It is found on chalk and limestone but also on nutrient-rich clays. It has spectacular autumn colour.

Its hard fine-grained wood has been used as a veneer, while the berries were eaten to cure colic. In the Weald of Kent and Sussex, wild service fruit is known as 'chequers' or 'chequer berries'. There are many pubs in this area called 'The Chequers' and it may

so the seeds may not be true wild service trees.

The fully ripe clusters of berries should be picked from the tree in September. Carefully remove the seeds from the flesh and wash thoroughly. Stratify the seed, usually for one winter. In cool

The shiny lobed leaves have their basal lobes at right angles to the leaf stalk. The rounded brown fruit is found in clusters.

Medium tree (6:12:20)

be that a drink was made from the berries or that they were added to beer.

Wild service berries provide good food for birds.

Seed Guide: Warning: wild service trees are prone to interbreed with many other Sorbus species,

autumns, germination can be improved by keeping stratifying seeds at room temperature for two weeks, before putting them outside for the winter. Select and sow germinating seeds in spring.

Easily confused with:
Field Maple and other Maples.

	JAN	FEB	MAR	APR	MAY	JUN	JUL	AUG	SEP	OCT	NOV	DEC
Year 1									Collect	Stratify		
Year 2			Sow	Grow						Plant		
Year 3												

Wild Cherry - *Prunus avium*

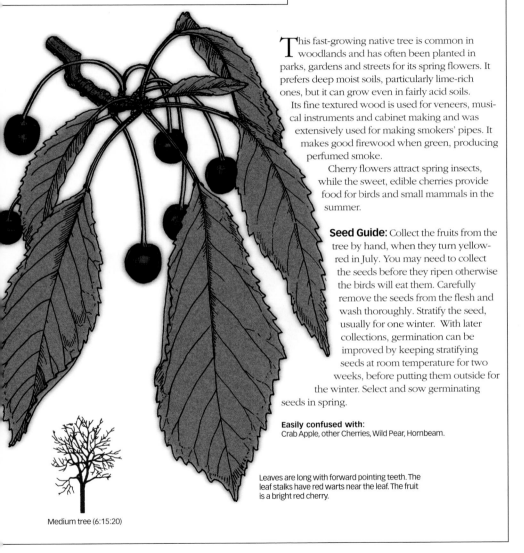

This fast-growing native tree is common in woodlands and has often been planted in parks, gardens and streets for its spring flowers. It prefers deep moist soils, particularly lime-rich ones, but it can grow even in fairly acid soils.

Its fine textured wood is used for veneers, musical instruments and cabinet making and was extensively used for making smokers' pipes. It makes good firewood when green, producing perfumed smoke.

Cherry flowers attract spring insects, while the sweet, edible cherries provide food for birds and small mammals in the summer.

Seed Guide: Collect the fruits from the tree by hand, when they turn yellow-red in July. You may need to collect the seeds before they ripen otherwise the birds will eat them. Carefully remove the seeds from the flesh and wash thoroughly. Stratify the seed, usually for one winter. With later collections, germination can be improved by keeping stratifying seeds at room temperature for two weeks, before putting them outside for the winter. Select and sow germinating seeds in spring.

Easily confused with:
Crab Apple, other Cherries, Wild Pear, Hornbeam.

Leaves are long with forward pointing teeth. The leaf stalks have red warts near the leaf. The fruit is a bright red cherry.

Medium tree (6:15:20)

	JAN	FEB	MAR	APR	MAY	JUN	JUL	AUG	SEP	OCT	NOV	DEC
Year 1							Collect	Stratify				
Year 2			Sow	Grow						Plant		
Year 3												

Bird Cherry - *Prunus padus*

The light-green leaves have fine, regular teeth. The black cherries contain a single hard stone.

Bird cherry is found in the north and west, growing wild in Scotland, Ireland, Wales, northern England and parts of the Midlands. It is most widespread by limestone streams in the Scottish glens, the Lake District and the Pennines. It has been grown in the south of England in streets and gardens for its attractive white flowers.

The reddish-brown heartwood was used in cabinet making and wood turning, whilst extracts from the bark were used for medicinal purposes. The bitter black cherries were also used to flavour brandies and wines.

Its outstanding flowers in May provide food for many insect species and its cherries are eaten by many birds and small mammals in the summer.

Seed Guide: Collect the fruits from the tree by hand when they turn black. Carefully remove the seeds from the flesh and wash thoroughly. Stratify the seed, usually for one winter. With later collections, germination can be improved by keeping stratifying seeds at room temperature for two weeks, before putting them outside for the winter. Select and sow germinating seeds in spring.

Easily confused with:
Crab Apple, other Cherries, Wild Pear, Hornbeam.

Medium tree (5:10:15)

	JAN	FEB	MAR	APR	MAY	JUN	JUL	AUG	SEP	OCT	NOV	DEC
Year 1							Collect		Stratify			
Year 2			Sow	Grow						Plant		
Year 3												

Blackthorn - *Prunus spinosa*

Shrub or small tree.

Small dull green leaves grow on dark thorny twigs. The blue-black sloes are very distinctive.

This widespread shrubby species can often be found on woodland edges and occurs on a wide range of soils. It sometimes grows into a small tree and its spiny twigs make it a good hedging plant.

The wood can be turned into walking sticks or, in Ireland, into a cudgel known as a shillelagh. The blue-black berries, known as sloes, are used to flavour gin or can be made into jam.

The species produces early flowers, which attract flying insects. The black hairstreak butterfly caterpillar feeds on the leaves.

Seed Guide: Collect the fruit (sloes) from the bush after the leaves have fallen. Remove the seeds from the flesh and wash thoroughly. Stratify the seed, usually for one winter. In cool autumns, germination can be improved by keeping stratifying seeds at room temperature for two weeks, before putting them outside for the winter. Select and sow germinating seeds in spring.

Easily confused with:
Crab Apple.

	JAN	FEB	MAR	APR	MAY	JUN	JUL	AUG	SEP	OCT	NOV	DEC
ar 1									Collect	Stratify		
ar 2			Sow	Grow						Plant		
ar 3												

Buckthorn - *Rhamnus catharticus*

The buckthorn is a shrub of the chalk and limestone of southern and central England. It grows in hedgerows or as scrub on downland and can occasionally form into small trees.

Historically the wood was used in making charcoal. Another name for the species is the purging buckthorn, in reference to the use of the inner bark and berries to create a violent purgative.

Buckthorn is one of the favoured foodplants of the brimstone butterfly and the berries are eaten by birds.

Seed Guide: To beat the birds, collect the fruits before they are fully ripe (i.e. completely black). Remove seeds from the fruit and wash thoroughly. Stratify the seed, usually for one winter, occasionally two. Select and sow germinating seeds in spring.

Easily confused with:
Alder Buckthorn.

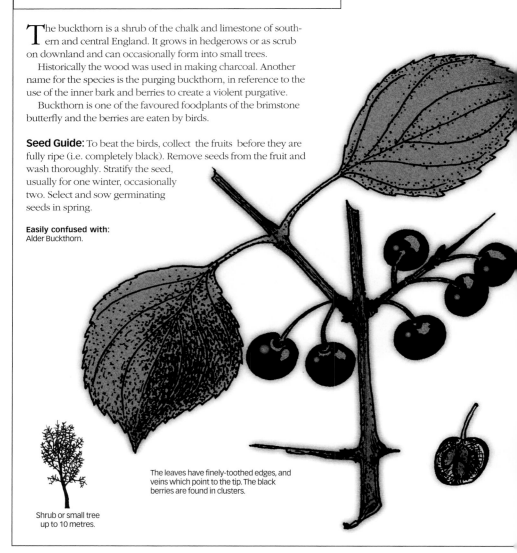

The leaves have finely-toothed edges, and veins which point to the tip. The black berries are found in clusters.

Shrub or small tree up to 10 metres.

	JAN	FEB	MAR	APR	MAY	JUN	JUL	AUG	SEP	OCT	NOV	DEC
Year 1									Collect	Stratify		
Year 2		Sow		Grow						Plant		
Year 3												

Alder Buckthorn - *Frangula alnus*

The shiny, untoothed leaves have 7-9 veins. The berries turn from green to red, then purple-black.

The alder buckthorn is a shrub or small tree which grows on peaty soils in damp woods and bogs. It is not related to either alder or buckthorn, but can be found growing with alder in wet woodlands. It has attractive autumn colours.

This species had a wide range of uses. The wood was used to prepare explosive fuses and charcoal, due to its slow-burning nature. Its berries, which ripen from green to red to black, were used for dyes and also as a purgative, along with its bark.

The tree is a food plant for the brimstone butterfly.

Seed Guide: Collect the fruits before they are fully ripe from late summer to early autumn. Remove seeds from the fruit and wash thoroughly. Stratify the seed, usually for one winter, occasionally two. Select and sow germinating seeds in spring.

Easily confused with:
Buckthorn.

Shrub or small tree up to 5 metres.

	JAN	FEB	MAR	APR	MAY	JUN	JUL	AUG	SEP	OCT	NOV	DEC
ear 1									Collect		Stratify	
ear 2			Sow	Grow						Plant		
ear 3												

Black Mulberry *Morus nigra*

Small tree (3:5:10)

The large heart-shaped leaves are hairy on both sides. The fruit is a deep, wine-red colour when ripe.

The black mulberry has been widely planted in southern England for its fruit but becomes rarer as one travels north. It originated in Asia and was first introduced to Britain in the 14th Century. In 1609, King James 1 increased the number planted in Britain in order to build up the silk industry, in the mistaken belief that silkworms fed on the leaves of the tree. In fact, silkworms favour the white mulberry (Morus alba), which does not appear to like the British climate greatly and remains uncommon.

The black mulberry grows well in parks and gardens and can be grown from seed. However, the more commonly used way of growing new trees is to take a 'truncheon' - a two-metre length of branch - which is driven one metre into the ground. It will then sprout to produce a new tree.

The wood is hard and valued for furniture and veneers, but it is a scarce wood and little used. The large, black raspberry-like fruits are tasty to humans and birds alike.

Seed Guide: Black mulberries are a similar shape and colour to raspberries. They fall from the tree when they are ripe and should be collected quickly before they are eaten by birds and animals. Squeeze the incredibly sticky fruits in your hand to release the seeds and wash thoroughly. Stratify the seed, usually for one winter, and inspect regularly. Select and sow germinating seeds from late winter onwards.

Easily confused with:
Elm, Hazel, Lime.

	JAN	FEB	MAR	APR	MAY	JUN	JUL	AUG	SEP	OCT	NOV	DEC
Year 1							Collect		Stratify			
Year 2		Sow	Grow							Plant		
Year 3												

Elder *Sambucus nigra*

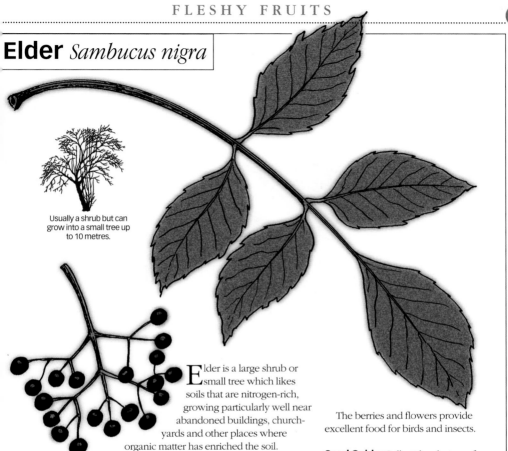

Usually a shrub but can grow into a small tree up to 10 metres.

The leaves consist of 5-7 toothed leaflets, which smell unpleasant. The black berries develop in clusters.

Elder is a large shrub or small tree which likes soils that are nitrogen-rich, growing particularly well near abandoned buildings, churchyards and other places where organic matter has enriched the soil.

If allowed to grow into a mature tree, the tree has hard wood, which was used for pegs and toys or, occasionally, for cogs in mills when hornbeam was not available.

The flowers and berries have a wide range of culinary uses, being made into wines or jams. The flower buds can be pickled or fried in batter, or infused as a drink. Various dyes can be made from parts of the tree, while the leaves can be made into an insecticide.

The berries and flowers provide excellent food for birds and insects.

Seed Guide: Collect the clusters of berries from the tree when they turn dark purple to black in August-October. Carefully squeeze the fruits to release the seeds. Then remove the seeds from the flesh and wash thoroughly. Stratify the seed, occasionally for one winter, but often two. Select and sow germinating seeds in spring.

Easily confused with:
Ash, Rowan, Walnut.

	JAN	FEB	MAR	APR	MAY	JUN	JUL	AUG	SEP	OCT	NOV	DEC
Year 1								Collect		Stratify		
Year 2			CHECK	CHECK								
Year 3			Sow	Grow						Plant		
Year 4												

Crab Apple *Malus sylvestris*

Easily confused with:
Cherry, Wild Pear.

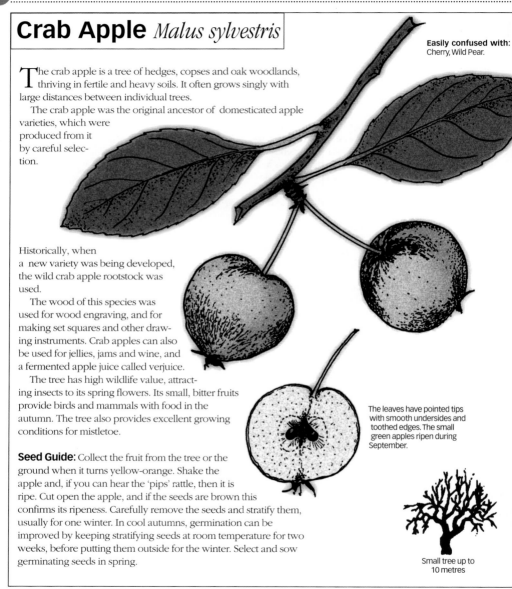

The crab apple is a tree of hedges, copses and oak woodlands, thriving in fertile and heavy soils. It often grows singly with large distances between individual trees.

The crab apple was the original ancestor of domesticated apple varieties, which were produced from it by careful selection.

Historically, when a new variety was being developed, the wild crab apple rootstock was used.

The wood of this species was used for wood engraving, and for making set squares and other drawing instruments. Crab apples can also be used for jellies, jams and wine, and a fermented apple juice called verjuice.

The tree has high wildlife value, attracting insects to its spring flowers. Its small, bitter fruits provide birds and mammals with food in the autumn. The tree also provides excellent growing conditions for mistletoe.

The leaves have pointed tips with smooth undersides and toothed edges. The small green apples ripen during September.

Seed Guide: Collect the fruit from the tree or the ground when it turns yellow-orange. Shake the apple and, if you can hear the 'pips' rattle, then it is ripe. Cut open the apple, and if the seeds are brown this confirms its ripeness. Carefully remove the seeds and stratify them, usually for one winter. In cool autumns, germination can be improved by keeping stratifying seeds at room temperature for two weeks, before putting them outside for the winter. Select and sow germinating seeds in spring.

Small tree up to 10 metres

	JAN	FEB	MAR	APR	MAY	JUN	JUL	AUG	SEP	OCT	NOV	DEC
Year 1									Collect		Stratify	
Year 2			Sow	Grow						Plant		
Year 3												

Wild Pear *Pyrus communis*

The wild pear can be found scattered alongside road verges, in hedgerows and on woodland edges throughout the country. It is also planted in parks and gardens. It is an uncommon tree, and may actually be rare, as many supposed wild pears are actually 'wildings' - trees descended from domesticated pears. The wild tree has spiny branches and produces small gritty pears. The dark brown bark also cracks into distinctive plates.

The pale pink wood takes stain easily and was used for veneers, wood turning, carving and for making musical instruments, including flutes and - when stained - black piano keys.

The flowers of wild pear attract insects in the spring, although to the human nose they smell fishy. The tree also provides excellent growing conditions for mistletoe.

Medium tree up to 15 metres.

The dark glossy leaves have smaller teeth than crab apples, with a longer leaf stalk.

Seed Guide: Collect the fruit from the tree or the ground when ripe. Cut open the pear, and if the seeds are brown this confirms that they are ripe. Carefully remove the seeds and stratify them, usually for one winter. In cool autumns, germination can be improved by keeping stratifying seeds at room temperature for two weeks, before putting them outside for the winter. Select and sow germinating seeds in spring.

Easily confused with:
Crab apple, Cherry.

	JAN	FEB	MAR	APR	MAY	JUN	JUL	AUG	SEP	OCT	NOV	DEC
ear 1										Collect	Stratify	
ear 2			Sow	Grow						Plant		
ear 3												

Ash *Fraxinus excelsior*

The ash is a very widespread woodland native tree growing throughout Britain, preferring moist, well-drained and fertile soils. Large, spreading ash trees can often be seen in hedgerows but, as it lacks much autumn colour, it is now infrequently planted in parks and gardens. A mature ash can produce 100,000 seeds.

Its strong wood is flexible and was used as an element in wheel making, for skis, oars and tool handles. It is still used for high-quality furniture.

It is a species with a high wildlife value, as it is used as a nesting site by woodpeckers and other hole-nesters, including redstarts. The tree also supports up to 68 species of invertebrates and over 200 species of lichen.

Seed Guide: Clusters of ash fruits are known as 'keys'. Wait until they have turned brown before collecting them from the tree. Separate the individual keys and stratify for at least two winters. Protect from predators and severe frost. Select and sow germinating seeds in early spring of the second and successive years.

Easily confused with:
Elder, Rowan, Walnut.

The leaves have 9-13 pairs of stalked leaflets with a single terminal leaflet. The single seeds have a long wing.

Large tree (6:10:25)

	JAN	FEB	MAR	APR	MAY	JUN	JUL	AUG	SEP	OCT	NOV	DEC
Year 1									Collect			Stratify
Year 2			CHECK	CHECK								
Year 3			Sow	Grow						Plant		
Year 4												

Field Maple *Acer campestre*

Medium tree (6:10:15)

Britain's only native maple, the field maple is a species which prefers lime-rich soil, but will tolerate other conditions. It occurs naturally in hedges and as the understorey in woods and copses throughout England and Wales. It is often grown in parks and gardens because of its beautiful autumn colour and its ability to tolerate air pollution. In the past, it was used for topiary.

The wood of the field maple is soft but produces beautiful veneer, used for wood turning and furniture. Historically, it was also used to make harps.

It is an important habitat for up to 51 invertebrate species, the plumed prominent moth being the most characteristic of these. The fruit 'keys' are often eaten by small mammals.

Seed Guide: Collect the fruits from the tree in autumn when they are brown. Stratify the seed, usually for one winter. Select and sow germinating seeds in spring.

Easily confused with: Hawthorn, Sycamore.

The small leaves have three main lobes and two smaller basal lobes. The seeds come in pairs, that are joined together almost in a straight line, and may have pink tinges.

	JAN	FEB	MAR	APR	MAY	JUN	JUL	AUG	SEP	OCT	NOV	DEC
ear 1										Collect	Stratify	
ear 2			Sow	Grow						Plant		
ear 3												

Sycamore *Acer pseudoplatanus*

This introduced species grows in a wide range of habitats and soil types. Sycamore is an excellent coloniser and is often considered a problem species as, in certain habitats, including woodland, it can become the dominant species.

Sycamore wood is light in colour, strong and hard, and is used for kitchen table-tops, flooring, veneers and toys.

This species supports a limited number of insect species, which includes large numbers of aphids. In consequence, migrating warblers can often be found feeding in sycamores in the autumn. The tree also supports good lichen growth, particularly in the west of Britain.

Seed Guide: Collect the fruits from the tree in autumn when they turn brown. Do not let the fruits dry out, or they will die. Stratify the seed for one winter. Select and sow germinating seeds in spring. Alternatively, sow immediately in a pot or seedbed; protect from predators and severe frost.

Easily confused with:
Field Maple and other Maples.

Large tree (10:15:25)

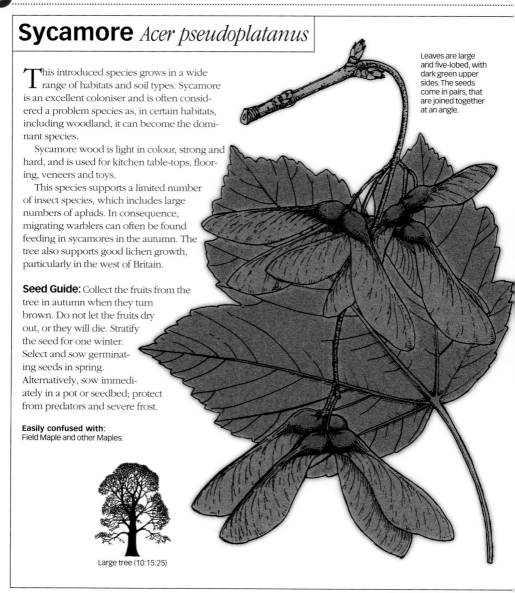

Leaves are large and five-lobed, with dark green upper sides. The seeds come in pairs, that are joined together at an angle.

	JAN	FEB	MAR	APR	MAY	JUN	JUL	AUG	SEP	OCT	NOV	DEC
Year 1									Collect		Stratify	
Year 2			Sow	Grow						Plant		
Year 3												

Hornbeam *Carpinus betulus*

Hornbeams are native trees found largely in south-eastern England, with scattered trees in other parts of the country. They tolerate a wide range of soils, including sands, gravels and heavy clay, but grow best on damp, fertile soils. Hornbeams produce excellent autumn colours, retaining their leaves throughout much of the winter.

Large tree (5:10:25)

One of the hardest and toughest woods in Britain, the name hornbeam derives from the fact that the wood is as hard as horn. It was used for cattle yokes, waterwheels and butchers' chopping blocks. The timber also makes excellent firewood.

Hornbeams are valuable to wildlife, producing nutlets which are eaten by hawfinches and small mammals. Over 50 species of invertebrates have been found feeding on this tree.

Seed Guide: Hornbeam fruits are a very unusual shape. Each heart-shaped fruit is attached to a leafy three-lobed structure known as a bract, which assists wind-dispersal. Collect the fruits by hand from the tree after the bracts have turned brown. Stratify the seed, usually for one winter. Select and sow germinating seeds in spring.

Easily confused with:
Beech, Wild Cherry, Bird Cherry, Wych Elm.

The reddish-stalked, toothed-edge leaves have pairs of prominent veins (10-15 pairs). The triangular nutlets grow in clusters of eight, each with a leafy three-lobed bract.

	JAN	FEB	MAR	APR	MAY	JUN	JUL	AUG	SEP	OCT	NOV	DEC
ear 1											Collect	Stratify
ear 2			Sow	Grow						Plant		
ear 3												

Common lime *Tilia x vulgaris*

The origins of this tree are uncertain and it is thought that it may be a hybrid between small-leaved and large-leaved lime. It appears the tree may have first been planted in the early 17th century, probably from European stock.

Now it is widely planted in streets, parks and gardens on a wide range of soils although it prefers soil that contains lime. However, it is not always the most suitable street tree, because it drips sticky sap onto cars in the summer, and produces large quantities of basal shoots, which may need annual maintenance.

Like the other two species of lime, the wood was used for carving and clogs, while the under or inner bark (bast) was turned into rope.

This tree, like the other limes, is excellent for wildlife, hosting 31 insect species, and frequently supports a growth of mistletoe. Unlike the other two limes, the seed of this species is rarely fertile.

Seed Guide: Lime fruits are a very unusual shape. The clusters of round fruits are attached via stalks to a single, leaf-like bract, which assists wind-dispersal. Collect the fruits by hand from the tree after the bracts have turned brown, usually following a frost. Stratify the seed for one or two winters. Select and sow germinating seeds in spring.

Easily confused with:
Elm, Hazel, Mulberry and other Limes.

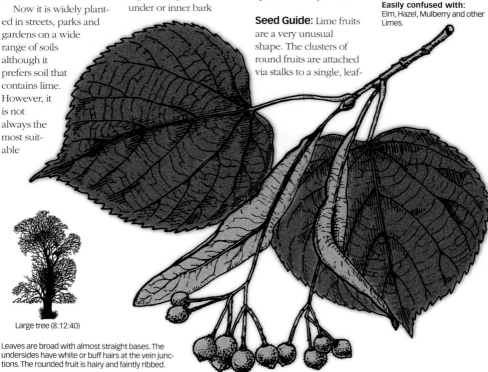

Large tree (8:12:40)

Leaves are broad with almost straight bases. The undersides have white or buff hairs at the vein junctions. The rounded fruit is hairy and faintly ribbed.

	JAN	FEB	MAR	APR	MAY	JUN	JUL	AUG	SEP	OCT	NOV	DEC
Year 1										Collect	Stratify	
Year 2			CHECK	CHECK								
Year 3			Sow	Grow						Plant		
Year 4												

Large-leaved lime *Tilia platyphyllos*

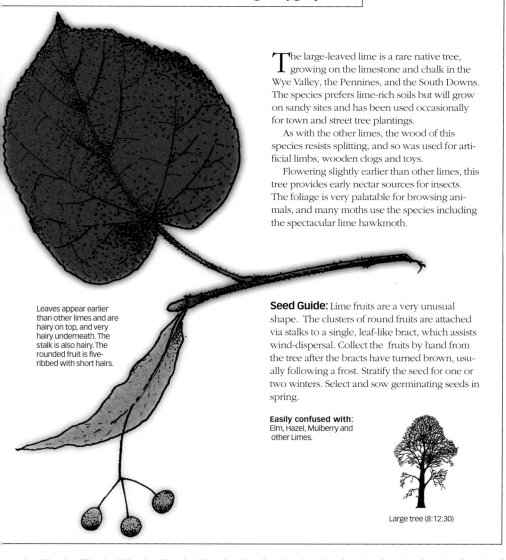

The large-leaved lime is a rare native tree, growing on the limestone and chalk in the Wye Valley, the Pennines, and the South Downs. The species prefers lime-rich soils but will grow on sandy sites and has been used occasionally for town and street tree plantings.

As with the other limes, the wood of this species resists splitting, and so was used for artificial limbs, wooden clogs and toys.

Flowering slightly earlier than other limes, this tree provides early nectar sources for insects. The foliage is very palatable for browsing animals, and many moths use the species including the spectacular lime hawkmoth.

Leaves appear earlier than other limes and are hairy on top, and very hairy underneath. The stalk is also hairy. The rounded fruit is five-ribbed with short hairs.

Seed Guide: Lime fruits are a very unusual shape. The clusters of round fruits are attached via stalks to a single, leaf-like bract, which assists wind-dispersal. Collect the fruits by hand from the tree after the bracts have turned brown, usually following a frost. Stratify the seed for one or two winters. Select and sow germinating seeds in spring.

Easily confused with:
Elm, Hazel, Mulberry and other Limes.

Large tree (8:12:30)

	JAN	FEB	MAR	APR	MAY	JUN	JUL	AUG	SEP	OCT	NOV	DEC
ar 1										Collect	Stratify	
ar 2			CHECK	CHECK								
ar 3			Sow	Grow						Plant		
ar 4												

Small-leaved lime *Tilia cordata*

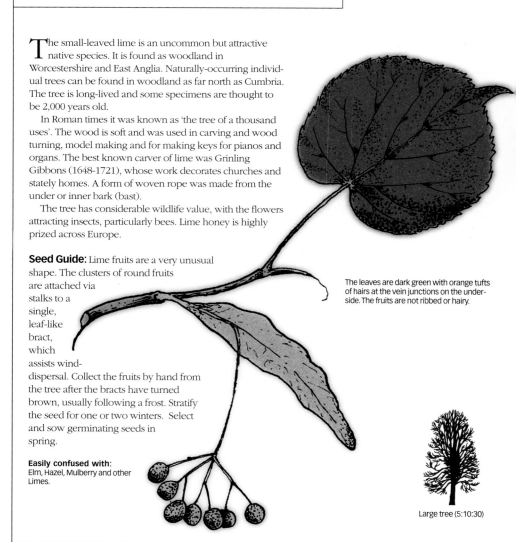

The small-leaved lime is an uncommon but attractive native species. It is found as woodland in Worcestershire and East Anglia. Naturally-occurring individual trees can be found in woodland as far north as Cumbria. The tree is long-lived and some specimens are thought to be 2,000 years old.

In Roman times it was known as 'the tree of a thousand uses'. The wood is soft and was used in carving and wood turning, model making and for making keys for pianos and organs. The best known carver of lime was Grinling Gibbons (1648-1721), whose work decorates churches and stately homes. A form of woven rope was made from the under or inner bark (bast).

The tree has considerable wildlife value, with the flowers attracting insects, particularly bees. Lime honey is highly prized across Europe.

Seed Guide: Lime fruits are a very unusual shape. The clusters of round fruits are attached via stalks to a single, leaf-like bract, which assists wind-dispersal. Collect the fruits by hand from the tree after the bracts have turned brown, usually following a frost. Stratify the seed for one or two winters. Select and sow germinating seeds in spring.

Easily confused with:
Elm, Hazel, Mulberry and other Limes.

The leaves are dark green with orange tufts of hairs at the vein junctions on the underside. The fruits are not ribbed or hairy.

Large tree (5:10:30)

	JAN	FEB	MAR	APR	MAY	JUN	JUL	AUG	SEP	OCT	NOV	DEC
Year 1										Collect	Stratify	
Year 2			CHECK	CHECK								
Year 3			Sow	Grow						Plant		
Year 4												

Wych Elm *Ulmus glabra*

The rough hairy leaves have an unequal base and strong teeth around the margin. The leaves also turn a distinctive yellow in autumn. The seed is set in the centre of the fruit.

The native wych elm is commonly found in hillside woods in Scotland, but is much less common in the south of Britain. Like other elms, this species has suffered from Dutch elm disease and its population is much reduced. It prefers growing on heavy moist clays and loams but will grow on chalk soils.

The fact that its wood is tough, even when wet, led to its use in making boats and for underground water pipes. Like other elms, it was also used to make wheel hubs, as the wood resists splitting.

White-letter hairstreak butterflies lay their eggs on this tree. Up to 81 other species of invertebrates have been recorded on the tree.

Seed Guide: Collect the fruits from the tree when the wings begin to turn brown in May/June. The winged fruits can be sown immediately into seed-trays. A small percentage will germinate quite quickly; however, many fruits are empty of seed and therefore will never germinate. Keep well watered and shaded in hot weather. Prick out seedlings into final containers. May need to be grown for two years.

Easily confused with :
Hazel, Lime, Mulberry, Hornbeam.

Large tree, up to 40 metres.

	JAN	FEB	MAR	APR	MAY	JUN	JUL	AUG	SEP	OCT	NOV	DEC
ear 1					Collect		Sow Grow					
ear 2										Plant		
ear 3												

Scots Pine *Pinus sylvestris*

The Scots pine is the only native pine in Britain, most widespread in Scotland, where there are extensive stands of old trees, especially in the Spey Valley and Upper Dee areas. It can also now be found on heathlands in the south of England, though this may be a later introduction. It grows on a wide range of soils, but prefers light and dry sands and gravels.

Scots pine produces strong, moderately hard wood that was used for charcoal and telegraph poles, and is still used for doors, floors and furniture.

The tree has excellent wildlife value, with 172 invertebrate species, including the pine hawkmoth, feeding on it. In Scottish pinewoods, it provides nesting sites for ospreys and Scottish crossbills, and the cones provide food for red squirrels which, in turn, are eaten by the rare pine marten.

Seed Guide: Scots pine cones can be collected from the lower branches of trees when they have turned from green to brown (Oct–Jan). Keep the cones in a paper bag or on a dish, at room temperature, to air-dry them. This causes them to open and release their seeds, which can be sown immediately. Cover with a thin layer of sharp sand and leave over winter to germinate the following spring.

The paired needles are usually twisted. The cones ripen over three years from green to brown, when the seeds are shed.

Large tree (8:12:35)

	JAN	FEB	MAR	APR	MAY	JUN	JUL	AUG	SEP	OCT	NOV	DEC
Year 1										Collect		
										Sow		
Year 2			Grow							Plant		
Year 3												

Common Alder *Alnus glutinosa*

This native alder grows in wet places, particularly wet clays, on marshes and by lakes and fens. It is able to survive in these sites, which generally lack the nitrates needed for growth, as its roots have nodules which contain nitrogen-fixing bacteria that extract nitrogen from the air.

The timber of alder was highly valued as, unlike many woods, it does not rot quickly when exposed to continual wetting and drying. In consequence, sluice gates and canal fittings like locks and gates were made from alder. Alder wood was also made into charcoal and used in the manufacture of gunpowder.

The tree has a high conservation value as the seeds provide good winter food for redpoll, siskins and other seed eaters. There are also up to 141 invertebrate species which feed on alder trees.

Seed Guide: Alder cones can be collected from the lower branches of trees before they open. Place cones in a paper bag and allow to air-dry at room temperature. As the cones open they will release the small winged seeds which can be sown immediately. Cover with a thin layer of sharp sand, and leave over winter to germinate the following spring.

Easily confused with:
Birch, Hornbeam, Lime.

The rounded leaves often have a notch at the tip and have seven pairs of distinctive white veins underneath. The female fruit is a green cone which turns black after the seed is shed.

Medium tree (8:15:20)

	JAN	FEB	MAR	APR	MAY	JUN	JUL	AUG	SEP	OCT	NOV	DEC
ear 1									Collect			
									Sow			
ear 2			Grow							Plant		
ear 3												

Silver Birch *Betula pendula*

The white-barked silver birch prefers drier conditions than downy birch, and is most widespread in the south and east of Britain, on light dry soils. It grows on heathlands, woodlands and is often planted in gardens and parks. A mature birch can produce up to one million seeds.

The strong white wood was used for bobbins, flooring and schoolmasters' canes. The bark was used for paper, shoes and roofing. Current uses include parquet floors, backing for veneers, furniture and broom handles.

Birch has a high conservation value as it provides food and shelter for a wide range of birds including redpolls and siskins. Up to 334 invertebrate species have been recorded in birches.

Seed Guide:

Birch cones can be collected from the lower branches of trees. Place the cones in a paper bag and allow them to dry at room temperature. Ripe cones will disintegrate on drying leaving a mixture of tiny winged seeds plus fleur-de-lys shaped bracts. Don't bother trying to separate them! The tiny seeds can be sown immediately and should be covered by a thin layer of sharp sand and left over winter until they germinate the following spring.

Easily confused with:
Downy Birch

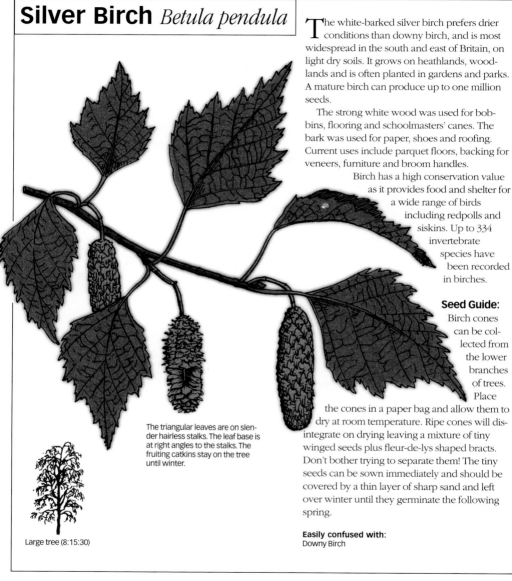

The triangular leaves are on slender hairless stalks. The leaf base is at right angles to the stalks. The fruiting catkins stay on the tree until winter.

Large tree (8:15:30)

	JAN	FEB	MAR	APR	MAY	JUN	JUL	AUG	SEP	OCT	NOV	DEC
Year 1								Collect				
								Sow				
Year 2			Grow							Plant		
Year 3												

Downy Birch *Betula pubescens*

The downy birch prefers wetter conditions than silver birch and is most widespread in the north and west of Britain, on poorly drained soils. Its bark is often darker than the silver birch, particularly at its base.

The wood of this tree was used to make furniture and veneers, while the branches were used to make besom brooms. The sugary sap, drawn from this and the silver birch, is used to produce birch wine, while oils from the bark can be used as an insect repellent.

As with silver birch, downy birch is excellent for wildlife, and again provides food for birds including black grouse, which can sometimes be seen feeding on the young catkins. Up to 334 invertebrate species have been recorded in birches.

Seed Guide: Birch cones can be collected from the lower branches of trees. Place the cones in a paper bag and allow them to dry at room temperature. Ripe cones will disintegrate on drying leaving a mixture of tiny winged seeds plus fleur-de-lys shaped bracts. Don't bother trying to separate them! The tiny seeds can be sown immediately and should be covered by a thin layer of sharp sand and left over winter until they germinate the following spring.

Easily confused with:
Silver birch

These leaves have hairy stalks and bases that are triangular. The teeth on the edges of the leaves are more regular than on silver birch. The fruiting catkins stay on the tree until winter.

Large tree (8:15:30)

	JAN	FEB	MAR	APR	MAY	JUN	JUL	AUG	SEP	OCT	NOV	DEC
ear 1								Collect				
								Sow				
ear 2			Grow							Plant		
ear 3												

Willows

There are 19 species of willow which are native to Britain. They are a difficult group of trees to separate because they can all breed with each other to create hybrid species. On these two pages are some of the more commonly found willow species. They species are not usually grown from seed, but from cuttings. (see p. 58)

Grey Willow
Salix cinerea

This many-branched shrub or small tree has two main sub-species - grey sallow and rusty sallow. This species is the commonest British willow, being found throughout the country.

Medium tree (10:15:15)

White Willow *Salix alba*

This willow species is a large tree, which grows beside rivers and ponds in low-altitude parts of the country. The cricket bat willow is a form of white willow, grown to produce cricket bats.

Medium tree (10:15:25)

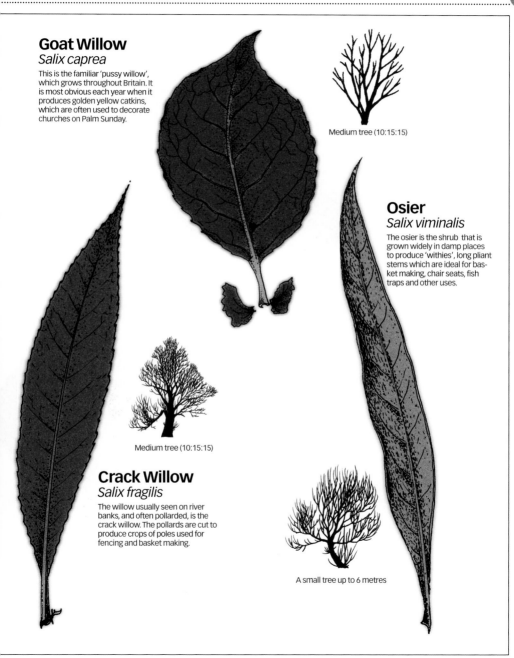

Goat Willow
Salix caprea

This is the familiar 'pussy willow', which grows throughout Britain. It is most obvious each year when it produces golden yellow catkins, which are often used to decorate churches on Palm Sunday.

Medium tree (10:15:15)

Osier
Salix viminalis

The osier is the shrub that is grown widely in damp places to produce 'withies', long pliant stems which are ideal for basket making, chair seats, fish traps and other uses.

Medium tree (10:15:15)

Crack Willow
Salix fragilis

The willow usually seen on river banks, and often pollarded, is the crack willow. The pollards are cut to produce crops of poles used for fencing and basket making.

A small tree up to 6 metres

Poplars

The poplars are fast growing trees, often reaching a large size. They have sticky buds and the male and females flowers are on separate trees. On these two pages are some of the more commonly found poplars. These species are not usually grown from seed, but from cuttings (see p.58).

Black Italian Poplar
Populus 'Serotina'

A commonly planted tree of the chalky south of Britain, this tree is a hybrid between the European black poplar and the American eastern cottonwood (Populus deltoides). It has been widely planted because it does not have the burred stem of its black poplar parent.

Large tree (10:15:30)

Black Poplar *Populus nigra*

The native black poplar is an uncommon tree which grows by slow-flowing water. This rare variety has a knobbly, burred stem and a distinctive leaning profile. Many other black poplar forms have been planted, among them the Lombardy poplar, which has an upright narrow form and is widely planted as a screen.

Large tree (10:15:30)

Large tree (10:15:30)

Grey Poplar *Populus canescens*

A hybrid between aspen and white poplar. It flourishes on damp ground such as water meadows and river valleys, and many large trees can be found in Hampshire and Dorset. Often mistaken for white poplar, the differences lie in the grey poplar's sturdy trunk and its darker foliage. Grey poplar is usually propagated from leafy, summer cuttings.

Aspen
Populus tremula

The aspen is a native tree found growing throughout Britain, although is most common in Scotland. The leaf stalk (petiole) is flattened which causes the leaves to tremble in the wind, producing a beautiful rustling sound.

A medium tree to a height of 20 metres

White Poplar
Populus alba

The white poplar is an introduced tree from southern Europe. It is found growing as shelter belts on river banks and is also used to stabilise sand dunes. The greyish white bark is marked by distinct black pores.

Medium tree (8:15:25)

Introduction

From the Seed to the Tree

The second section of this book is designed to show how to collect seeds and turn them into healthy young trees.

The following pages provide step-by-step guidance on collecting, handling, stratifying and germinating your seeds. This section shows you how to plant out seedlings once they have started to grow, and then how to ensure your young tree has the healthiest start in life.

Willows and poplars are actually better grown from cuttings than from their seeds. Full instructions about how to do this are also contained in this section.

Growing trees from seed is not complicated. Anyone can do it with a few simple pieces of equipment and it's a great way to put something back into your environment. Not every seed you plant will become a magnificent tree but, with care, many can. So good growing!

'The best time to plant a tree was twenty years ago. The second best time is now.'
– Anon

Quoted in *The Simple Act of Planting A Tree* by Andy and Katie Lipkis
[Tarcher Inc. Los Angeles. 1990]

Collecting Seeds

Very few trees produce good crops of seed every year. Keep an eye on the quality and quantity of seed developing on the parent trees. Check seeds are ripe by referring to the notes in Section 1 of the Guide before you collect them.

When ripe, the seeds should be picked directly from the tree, or gathered from the ground. Use a paper or hessian bag to take your seeds home. Don't use plastic bags as they may cause the seeds to become too moist, which will reduce their chances of germination. Put seeds from different species of trees in separate bags and label them.

The ideal situation is to collect seed from trees that are growing well in your area and are obviously suited to local conditions.

Do think carefully before collecting seeds hundreds of miles from where you will plant the tree. Trees do become adapted to their local conditions and seed collected in Sussex may not produce healthy trees in Perthshire.

If the trees are on private land, it is very important to ask the permission of the tree's owner before collecting any seed.

Don't collect the first seeds to fall from a tree, as later seed will probably be of better quality. Watch carefully as your seed ripens, for delaying too long may mean the squirrels, other animals and birds beat you to it! However, always leave some seeds, as they are an important food source for wildlife.

Climbing trees is dangerous, so only collect seed you can reach from the ground. Use gloves if you are collecting seed from spiny trees or bushes. If you want to collect seed from the lower branches of trees, pick them by hand or use a hooked stick to carefully pull branches down to within your reach.

Preparation

Most tree seeds are contained in some kind of fruit - apple pips and cherry stones are good examples - and they will first need to be extracted and cleaned. The method you should use depends on the type of fruit or seed you have collected - nuts, fleshy fruits, winged seeds or cones.

Once you have separated your seeds into types, you will know whether they need to be either stratified for the winter, or sown immediately into pots or seedbeds (see next page).

You will never get all of your seeds to germinate, but by using the following methods your chances of success can be greatly increased.

Fleshy Fruits

Mix the berries with water and then gently mash them with a potato masher or similar device. Viable seed will sink to the bottom and the residue of the fleshy fruit can be discarded. For rowan and mulberry, put the berries in a sieve and gently squeeze them with your fingers under running water to release the seeds. The seeds of all fleshy fruits need to be stratified.

Cones

Put your ripe cones in a paper bag to dry out naturally for a few days - but not in direct sunlight, or on a radiator, or by a fire. The cones will open up and release their seeds which will then be ready to be sown.

Nuts

For acorns and chestnuts, separate the nuts from their cups or outer casings and drop them into a bucket or bowl of water. Discard the ones that float and collect those that sink for sowing. Beech, walnut and hazel nuts should be stratified and then sown when they have germinated.

Winged seeds

Winged seeds can be planted with the wings left on. Separate the seeds from each other and from their twigs, then stratify. Of the species that we've have chosen, the only exception to this method is wych elm, which is collected in summer and should be sown immediately.

Stratification and Germination

Very few tree seeds will germinate (shoot or sprout) without exposure to the cold of at least one winter. Other species take even longer, needing the following summer plus another winter before showing signs of life. This is because of a natural defence mechanism built into the seeds, which ensures that they do not grow during the winter months when the young seedlings might be killed by the cold.

Tree growers have developed a technique called stratification which aims to mimic this natural process. To stratify your seeds, mix them with an equal volume of stratification medium (see caption for recipe) and put them in a pot or bucket which has holes in the bottom for drainage.

The container should then be covered with a fine wire-mesh lid, to keep out birds and rodents, and either buried in the ground, placed against a north-facing wall or kept in a cool outhouse.

It is essential to keep the mixture moist but not saturated. It's moist enough if you can squeeze out

a drop of water when you pinch the mixture between your thumb and forefinger.

In the spring, tip out the mixture and remove any seeds that are showing small shoots or roots. These seeds are germinating and are ready for sowing. Any seeds that haven't germinated should be put back into the stratification mixture. Keep checking the seeds weekly during the spring, sowing any that germinate.

Once the seeds are growing, it is important to sow them quickly, as the new shoots are fragile. If they get too large, they can be damaged during planting. If any seeds haven't germinated by the end of the spring, don't be disheartened. It is possible they may need two winters, but check that the seeds haven't rotted before continuing to stratify.

Choose whatever size containers you have to hand. The most important thing is to ensure that the tops are covered with fine wire mesh to prevent animals and birds from eating the seeds.

Stratification is a technique designed to mimic nature by exposing seeds to the cold of at least one winter. Germination is when seeds develop small shoots or roots.

A good recipe for a stratification mixture:	• Add one volume of peat-free potting compost (fresh or recycled) to an equal volume of a coarse-particle material, such as bark-chips, perlite, sand or grit.	• Then mix an equal volume of seeds and stratification mixture together and put in a pot, bucket or dustbin.

Sowing

Once you have cleaned and, if necessary, stratified your seeds they are ready for sowing. Sow your seeds in a suitable container - such as a milk carton or Rootrainer - or in an outdoor seedbed.

Small seeds like birch and alder should be sown on the surface of the compost or soil and covered with a thin layer of sharp sand. It is best to sow several small seeds (a pinch) in each container and then thin to leave the strongest seedlings. Larger seeds are usually sown singly and covered to about one-and-a half times their average length with soil or compost.

Wherever you sow your seeds, you will need to ensure that they don't get waterlogged. In containers, this can be achieved by ensuring that there are holes in the bottom. In outdoor seedbeds, digging in sand and grit may help improve drainage and prevent waterlogging in heavy soils.

Germinating seeds will need shelter from hot sun, cold winds, frost, birds, mice and other animals. A shady spot against a wall is ideal. Make sure you water your containers regularly, especially in the summer.

Occasionally give the seedlings some liquid plant feed and weed the containers and seedbeds - but make sure you avoid pulling up the young trees by mistake!

This is the ideal method for growing a single tree. First, cut off the top of your milk carton and then pierce small holes in the bottom to allow water to escape. Fill it with potting compost (preferably peat-free) and sow either a single germinating seed, or a pinch of small seeds. As the tree grows, water regularly to ensure the compost does not dry out. Feed during periods of active growth. After a few months the young tree may outgrow its pot, so the tree should be transferred to a larger container or planted out.

Rootrainers are small moulded plastic cells which come in hinged packs with four or five cells in each row, allowing you to open them up to examine how your young trees are developing. Five or six rows of these Rootrainer packs can be placed together in a tray, allowing twenty or more trees to be grown in a small space.

As with milk cartons, fill with potting compost (preferably peat-free) and sow either a single germinating seed, or a pinch of small seeds, in each one. As the trees grow, water regularly. Add plant feed during active growth. When the young trees have grown well-developed roots, they are ready to be planted out. (Rootrainers can be obtained from most garden centres and shops or from specialised stockists. (See Page 64)

A seedbed is a mini tree-nursery. To create one, first prepare the soil to ensure that it is free draining and if necessary add some coarse grit to the soil to improve drainage. Either sow your seeds over the surface of the seedbed before covering them with a layer of soil or sow in a drill - a shallow groove scraped out to the required depth - and re-cover with soil.

Use a protective fence to keep the rabbits and rodents away from your seeds and seedlings. As the young trees grow, ensure they are watered regularly. Trees growing in seed beds can be left for a year or more before being planted out.

Taking and Planting Cuttings

Trees such as willows and poplars grow better from cuttings than from seed. When seed is difficult to obtain, cuttings can also be taken from alder, elder, hazel, holly and mulberries. Generally, cuttings should be taken in late autumn or early winter.

These cuttings should be set upright in moist, well-drained soils. Poplars and willows root so readily that anyone can plant them with a good chance of success.

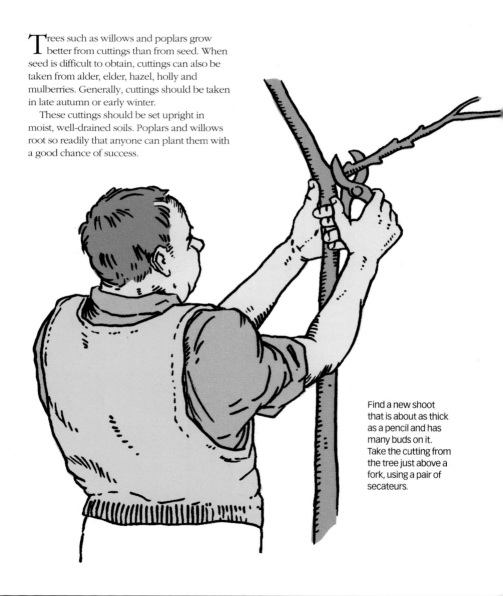

Find a new shoot that is about as thick as a pencil and has many buds on it. Take the cutting from the tree just above a fork, using a pair of secateurs.

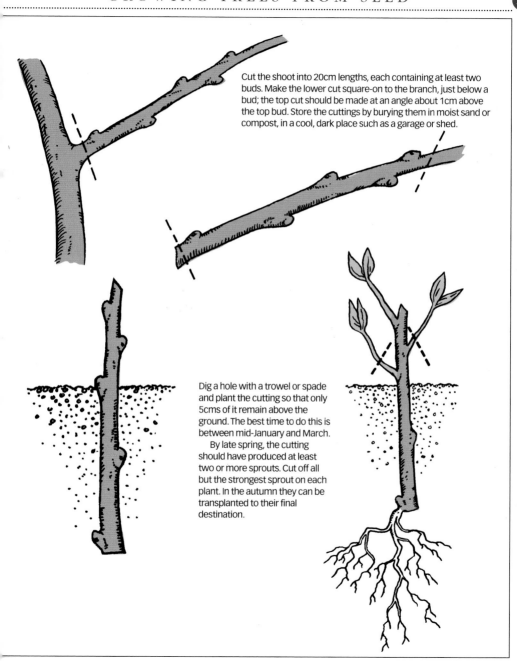

Cut the shoot into 20cm lengths, each containing at least two buds. Make the lower cut square-on to the branch, just below a bud; the top cut should be made at an angle about 1cm above the top bud. Store the cuttings by burying them in moist sand or compost, in a cool, dark place such as a garage or shed.

Dig a hole with a trowel or spade and plant the cutting so that only 5cms of it remain above the ground. The best time to do this is between mid-January and March.

By late spring, the cutting should have produced at least two or more sprouts. Cut off all but the strongest sprout on each plant. In the autumn they can be transplanted to their final destination.

Planting Out

When your seedlings have grown into small trees, they need to be transplanted to their final growing positions. This should be undertaken during the winter planting season, normally November to March.

There are many potential places where a tree can be planted including gardens, communal and public open space, road verges, parks, hedgerows, woodlands and churchyards. However, it is vital that you only plant a tree when you have the landowner's permission and ensure that there will be enough space for your tree when it reaches maturity.

Choose well-drained sites where the ground is not too hard. Test this by seeing whether you can push a trowel or spade into the ground simply by leaning on it.

If rabbits, squirrels, deer or livestock are found in the area, protect your tree from bark damage with a tree guard - essentially a plastic tube that fits round the stem. These guards also help to protect the tree against strimmers or lawnmowers. Guards come in many shapes and sizes, so make sure you buy one of the right size (see P.64 for stockists).

For small trees grown in cartons or Rootrainers, use a trowel to dig a hole for the tree. Ensure that the hole is deep enough to take all the soil and roots from the pots. If required, use a little extra compost or fine soil to pack around the tree.

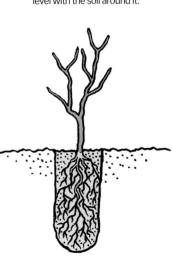

Carton: Moisten the compost before removing the tree from its carton. When planted, the surface of the soil from the pot should be level with the soil around it.

Rootrainer: Use essentially the same procedure as when planting from a carton. However, as the soil volume is smaller, these trees can also be planted by using a spade to make a slot in the ground. Widen it by wiggling the spade backwards and forwards and then put the tree and its soil in the centre of the slot. Carefully push the sides of the slot back together using your foot to close the slot and firm the soil around the tree.

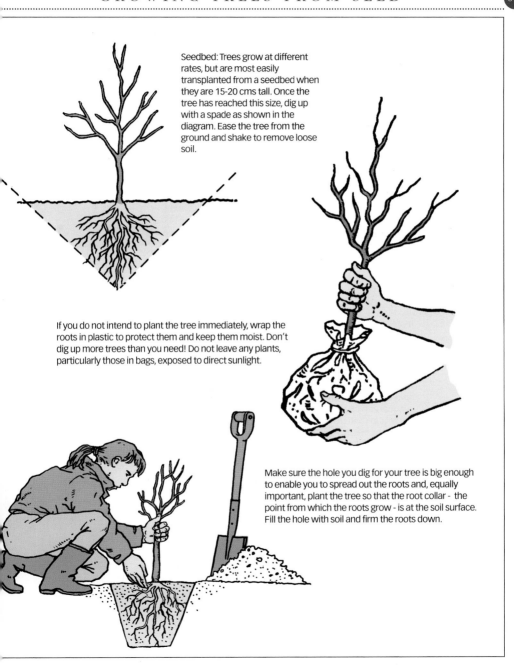

Seedbed: Trees grow at different rates, but are most easily transplanted from a seedbed when they are 15-20 cms tall. Once the tree has reached this size, dig up with a spade as shown in the diagram. Ease the tree from the ground and shake to remove loose soil.

If you do not intend to plant the tree immediately, wrap the roots in plastic to protect them and keep them moist. Don't dig up more trees than you need! Do not leave any plants, particularly those in bags, exposed to direct sunlight.

Make sure the hole you dig for your tree is big enough to enable you to spread out the roots and, equally important, plant the tree so that the root collar - the point from which the roots grow - is at the soil surface. Fill the hole with soil and firm the roots down.

Aftercare

When your tree has been planted in its permanent position, there are still a range of tasks that need to be undertaken to ensure it survives. Research has shown that 50% of newly planted trees may die in their first five years due to a lack of aftercare.

The Tree Council has therefore developed the TLC campaign to remind you of the three simple tasks that need to be undertaken at least once a year - between March and September - for the first five years, to ensure that your young tree survives and thrives.

TLC for young trees involves:
Tending the tree, checking its health, watering if necessary, making the tree firm in the ground if it has been rocked by the wind, and removing broken branches.
Loosening ties - small straps used to secure trees to stakes - to make sure they are not rubbing or chafing the tree, and checking the guard to make sure that it is still effective. (Small trees do not need stakes.)
Clearing all weeds and grasses from one square metre around the tree's base, and ensuring that the mulching is still effective.

Look at the guard that you have placed around the tree. Check that it is still intact and effectively protecting the tree. If not, replace it. Once the tree has become well-established, remove the guard entirely.

Young trees often die from lack of water particularly if they have to compete with surrounding grass. Cutting the grass only makes things worse as cut grass grows more vigorously. The solution is to create a one square metre weed-free area around the tree. To keep the area free of weeds, you can cover it with a 'mulch mat' or with bark chippings or other composted woody material.

Sometimes it is difficult to know whether your tree is alive or dead. To check, look for living buds or scrape a little bark from a twig - a live tree will be green beneath the bark, not brown. Branches that are broken or dead can be removed. Cut the branches off with a cut just away from the main stem.

Further information

Sources

Boulton, E. *British Timbers* (Black. 1944)

Brooks, M. *The Complete British Moths* (Cape. 1991)

Clapham, A. et al. *Flora of the British Isles* (Cambridge University Press. 1987)

Evelyn, John. *Sylva* (Original Edition. London. 1666)

Kiser, B. *Trees and Aftercare* (BTCV)

Gordon, A. and Rowe D. *Seed Manual for Ornamental Trees and Shrubs* (HMSO. 1982)

Grieve, M. A *Modern Herbal* (Penguin. 1984)

Grigson, G. *The Englishman's Flora* (Dent. 1987)

Heath, J., Pollard, E. and Thomas, K.A. *Atlas of Butterflies in Britain and Ireland* (Viking. 1984)

Lang, D. *The Complete Book of British Berries* (Threshold Books. 1987)

Mabey, Richard. *Flora Britannica* (Sinclair Stevenson. 1996)

Meikle, R. *Willows and Poplars of Great Britain and Ireland* (BSBI. 1984)

Milner, J. *The Tree Book* (Collins and Brown. 1982)

Mitchell, J. and Jobling, J. *Decorative Trees* (HMSO. 1984)

Mitchell, A. *Field Guide to the Trees of Britain and Northern Europe* (Collins. 1988)

Mitchell, A. *Trees of Britain* (Harper Collins. 1996)

Our trees: a guide to growing Northern Ireland's native trees from seed (CVNI. Belfast. 1996)

Strouts, R.G. and Winter, T.G. *Diagnosis of Ill-health in Trees* (HMSO. 1994)

White, J. *Forest and Woodland Trees in Britain* (Oxford. 1995)

Wilkinson, G. *Trees in the Wild* (Bartholemew.1973).

Further Reading/Tree Identification:

Miles, Archie. *Silva* (Ebury Press. 1999)

Packenham, Thomas. *Meetings with Remarkable Trees* (Weidenfield and Nicolson.1996)

The Readers Digest Book of Trees and Shrubs of Britain (Readers Digest. 1981)

Rushford, Keith. *The Mitchell Beazley Pocket Guide to Trees* (Mitchell Beazley. 1980/1990)

MacDonald, B. *Practical Woody Plant Propogation for Nursery Growers* (Batsford. 1986).

Rootrainer kits are available from:

Arid Lands Initiative, Machpelah Works, Burnley Road, Hebden Bridge, W. Yorks HX7 8AZ (Tel: 01422 843807) at around £15 for 24 cells. Similar plug trays are available from garden centres.

Tree Guards are available from garden centres and many individual companies including Tubex, Aberaman Park, Aberdare, Wales CF44 6DA. Tel: 01685 888000